JUST AN ORDINARY JOE

by

Joseph G. Gallucci Jr.

authorHOUSE™

1663 LIBERTY DRIVE, SUITE 200
BLOOMINGTON, INDIANA 47403
(800) 839-8640
WWW.AUTHORHOUSE.COM

First published by AuthorHouse 04/11/05

ISBN: 1-4208-2688-3 (sc)

Printed in the United States of America
Bloomington, Indiana

This book is printed on acid-free paper.

To my Cuchie Cu

AND

Anthony Joe

Session One

It was just an ordinary day for Joe. The day being a lovely affair, it was like a child refusing to give up its toy. It just wouldn't let the fall take over it's summer season.

Joe on the other hand, was grateful to his God for yet another glorious day of life. His term of service to the Lord was approaching its 63rd. year on earth, and Joe could really feel the years, as if they were barnacles clinging to a piece of driftwood floating in the vast ocean.

Joe awoke on this particular morning with a strong urge to review the dream that he had had the previous night, while enjoying his nocturnal interlude with sleep. Joe was not the type who would normally remember his dreams, as some often do. He always thought of his deceased mother in-law, who would frequently dream and than interpret her dreams into numbers. Consequently she would have her daily set of numbers to play with her ever present bookie on the street.

For some strange reason though, Joe could hardly wait to sit down to the computer and record his dream for future evaluation and consideration.

He quickly washed his face and hands, brushed his teeth, and then hurried to a quick breakfast, consisting of two slices of toast, then downed his daily vitamin and mineral supplemental pill.

All during the mundane tasks of morning, he could not curtail his excessive urge to go over and over the happenings he had so vividly dreamed. He was even hesitant to recall it, for fear of offending Almighty God.

Now as I'm sure the reader has surmised, Joe was a devout Roman Catholic with all the usual doctrines instilled from childhood. He was not as good a Catholic as he should have been, but hopefully felt he was doing his best. He had complete faith in Jesus, and truly trusted in Him for everything in his life.

Joe often regretted his lack of reciting the Rosary on a daily basis. He prayed fervently to the Blessed Mother, but just couldn't get himself to pray the long and repetitiously slow prayer. So here he was, Joe, a Catholic who did not even pray the Rosary but did receive the Body of Christ, each and every Sunday.

Hey! Wait a minute, what am I doing here? Writing an autobiography? Actually no, what I'm trying to accomplish is a fictitious novel. But wait a second, wouldn't it be unique if I incorporated my bio into the story? Yes, I believe this could work. Using my bio and my actual family and friends, in the telling of my story. Okay now that I've established that, let me first insert, right about here an elaborate bio which I have already started since 1996, and continue to add to periodically. That is when I get the urge to write, which isn't too often.

Actually, I think it would add to the length of the story as well as enhance the readers understanding of the hopeful author's make up.

Session Two

After numerous attempts to sit down and put to paper a legitimate novel, I've finally come to the conclusion that it is impossible to attain. (Goes to show how much I know). The reasons or rather the excuses that come to mind are varied. To list a few, I would have to say that researching a particular subject thoroughly is the most profoundly difficult and time consuming. To posses a knowledge of a specific topic and to achieve the goal of portraying to the reader an actual personality, realistically, is far beyond my capabilities. Gratefully though, I thank God for not being a quitter and for having the mentality and faith to figure out a solution to my problem.

It has come to me that I could try writing my own life story. It is a topic I'm familiar with and one that I am entirely knowledgeable of. Although my memory of various occurrences in my life may be less than accurate, I still feel it can be accomplished. Another factor which is propelling me towards this end, is the fact that I can leave this document as a legacy to my children and grandchildren. This idea came to me most vividly, after watching the movie "The Egyptian" on AMC TV. And so to proceed on this hopefully truthful journey let me first list some ground rules to my format. First, I've decided not to list my recollections in chronological order. I feel this will make for a more flavorful rendition. The length and/or brevity of the piece will have no boundaries. I will come back to this writing at various times in my life when I feel the urge or compelling feeling of writing come upon me. This I must do because God has blessed me with many interests to occupy my mental and physical body with. Now, before I begin, let me document the date and time of this quest. Today is Monday, January 29, 1996. The time of day at the start was approximately 5:15 P.M. Now, to quote Confucius, "The longest journey starts with a single step."

Session Three

The small eight by ten hallway was just adjacent to the D.I.'s room and leading to the main squad bay at the other end. The wooden parcade floor glistened with a high sheen which was applied to it during our all-day field day of the barracks. The imaginary dust specks that I was presumably wiping from the glossy floor were lovingly adhering to the damp mop I was bending over. I was bending over the mop in a precarious way, so as to incline my ears to the conversation which was taking place at the foot of the D.I.'s abode.

There, standing at rigid attention, in front of the Drill Instructor, was a brand new recruit. He must have been a few hours from an ordinary civilian. I heard him crying and saw tears running down his cheeks, as he muttered with frustration that he just couldn't do it. He just wanted to go home. The sight of him was hilarious. His over-sized utility cap was pulled down over his ears and covered his completely bald head. I was thinking to myself, "boy, this poor kid ain't seen nothing yet, just wait!" This was the day before my platoons' final graduation from Marine Corps Paris Island. We had started with sixty some odd recruits, and only ended with about forty five full fledged Marines. It was the most rigorous and stressful experience I had ever in my life encountered. I was so grateful to God for having me complete the training successfully. While these thoughts played happily in my mind, I was suddenly startled by the sound of my surname, "Gallucci!" I raised my body and mind instinctively and ran quickly to post myself in front of the D.I. Being just to the left of the new recruit, I bellowed out, "Sir, Private Gallucci reporting as ordered, Sir!" This was the regular format for a recruit to answer to a D.I., but surprising to me was the fact that he had called me by my name. That in itself was a huge compliment to me, since for the past 15 weeks, I, like all of my comrades were referred to by various monikers like shit head, civilian shit, maggot, turd, numbnuts, etc. Then he exclaimed in a harsh voice: "See Gallucci here, he was a numb nut, turd, civilian, shithead just about 15 weeks ago, but look at him now. He's a United States Marine. He can take and do anything. Ain't that right Gallucci?" Before the ucci came out of the D.I.'s mouth he had hit me with a one two punch, one to the stomach and the second to the jaw. I was dumb founded and mad at the same time. The slime thought of a reprisal punch to the D.I.'s face was quickly thwarted when I saw the look of shock on the recruit's face as he noticed that I had not even budged from the two hard blows. After reciting my "Yes sir," I was quickly dismissed.

Having been able to endure all the unyielding training at Paris Island was only a feather in my father's cap.

Session Four

Speaking of my father, I guess now is about the time to elaborate on him, since I'd have to sooner or later. Unfortunately I hated my father for most of my childhood. I was deathly afraid of him, and consequently stayed out of a lot more trouble than I might have gotten into, had I not feared him so.

I can vividly recall when I was a little boy, not recollecting the exact age, looking out my kitchen window. The window looked out our backyard, which was strewn with natural foliage. The reason for my spying from the window was because I was aroused by a loud whining and barking coming from my childhood love of my life, my dog, Blackie. He was a small, completely black haired mixed breed mutt. My two older sisters and I adored him. Later in my life story I will return to Blackie for another memorable event in my childhood.

Continuing with the incident of Blackie and my father, the terrible noise which emanated from the back yard was the screechingly loud cry of the dog. My father was brutally beating Blackie into submission for no apparent reason, other than to gain fear and respect out of the dog. Not till now do I realize Blackie could well have been me. This he certainly could do, and was a fact which was etched in my psyche for life.

My father did a lot of disappointing things to me as a child, but I can't blame him since he was so uneducated and materially poor. Later in life, especially when I became a father myself, I realized that he must have really loved me, since he would take so much time disciplining me as he did.

For instance I can remember, as if it were yesterday, when I cursed at a next door neighbor who wouldn't return my errant ball. The woman had promptly notified my father of the fact. The next thing I remember, I was cradled between my fathers legs and was having an old fashioned mouth washing, with much lather being applied to my mouth. I must note at this point that the expletive I used was calling her a f---ing whore. The reason I mention it is to tell you now that I am presently a man of 63 years, and I can't honestly recall when the last time I used that four letter word was.

My father had a vicious way about him, was quiet, strong and good hearted. To elaborate further on his brutality, I'll state here, that he often beat me and even my two older sisters when we did wrong. After this he would lock us in a dark closet. Oh, he did a lot of wild things to us, but never anything perverted. He was just an old fashioned disciplinarian, who loved his family very much. A shrink once told me that, "your father still controls your personality, even though he is dead." I don't know how true that is but I can attest to the fact that I was one of the 45 graduates from a class of 62 at Paris Island, South Carolina in 1958. Oh, before I get off the subject of my father, let me relate just one more tale about the last and only time I ever stole anything in my life.

Session Five

Flash, Flash! I will interrupt the continuation of this my life story at this time so that I may write about a most significant occurrence, the birth of my first grandson. He is the second wonderful grandchild God has bestowed on us and the first to carry on the Gallucci name. I thank God firstly for this wonderful gift and pray that He will always be with him, watching over him and guiding him in His ways. Please God, Let his love of You and faith in You be very strong. This I beg of Thee for him and all my family and friends, as well as myself. Amen.

His name is Anthony Joseph Gallucci. He was born at 5:30 PM on Wednesday, March 20th. 1996.

He was 6 pounds and 12 ounces in weight and 19 inches tall, a handsome little guy.

My first quest on his behalf will be to track down the whereabouts of a place that I can purchase a miniature U.S. Marine Corps uniform.

Its a good thing that I said I would not write this biography in chronological order. Ha! Ha! I will now get back to the next memorable occurrence in my life.

Session Six

Emergency- guess what just happened. After having completed 20 pages of text towards this my bio, I've inadvertently wiped out 15 pages of my writings. After a week of devastating anger and much assistance from knowledgeable people, I've come to the conclusion that I did commit an unforgivable blunder by not saving my daily work on floppy disk. And so rather than packing the whole thing in, I will endeavor to continue at my leisure in hopes that I can recapture what I've previously wrote. Not right now though, cause I'm still a little pissed. I'll now close today's session with a save to floppy and c drive.

Session Seven

Ready to start again, I will now continue at the point above where I was about to describe another of my father's actions against me.

It took place on the street of 122nd., between Pleasant and 1st Avenues, where I lived. It was a nice summer day and a few friends and myself were just hanging around in our old mischievous way. Just then, a big Coca Cola truck pulled up and parked directly across from us. The driver disembarked from his vehicle and proceeded to an old candy store, owned by the Pipilos. This wondrous place where we would often congregate stood at the precise center of our block.

As the driver was in the store taking his intriguing order from the proprietor, we in our roguish way decided to relieve our thirst. After all, the truck contained vast amounts of unprotected baubles of nectar. The bottles were just gleaming, waiting to be picked, as Eve did, in the garden of Eden. These delights were masked in the familiar green bottles of Coca Cola. Brazenly we all went over to the side of the truck which was hidden from the store front's view. Reaching up, we all plucked a variety of bottles.

When I myself had just touched a fine bottle, my efforts were thwarted by a firm hand which secured itself on the back of my neck. My mind raced with the thoughts of what and who could this be, applying such pressure to my neck? My mind came up with the right answer. In that split second I realized that it was approximately 4 P.M. the bewitching hour of my fathers return from work as a sanitation man.

As I strained to gaze upon my assailant, I was met by two piercing eyes and a mouth that vocalized the following; "get upstairs and wait for me." With absolute haste and trepidation, I obeyed this edict, and ran upstairs. I waited with much agony of anticipation for my sentence to befall me. After approximately only ten minutes, which to me felt like a lifetime, my father appeared. He did not utter a word but commenced immediately to beat the living shit out of me. In my vast experiences of street tussles, it was the most excruciating beating I had ever endured. I remember not being able to walk normally for a few days after.

From that day until this, I can honestly say I can't remember another occasion where I stole anything from anyone. Thanks Pop.

Session Eight

At this particular urging from our Lord, I've gotten the idea to include some religious writings. Some of these will be my own original words and some others from different authors. It will be a nice change of pace from the "myself" theme of the writings and also a chance for the reader to better know and love their God.

So now, accept a rendition of a short story from Just an Ordinary Joe. The idea for it came from an old Marine Corps buddy.

The Solution...........by Joe Gallucci

The room was huge and silent as a great hush came over its entirety. The bald headed scientist, wearing the thick bifocals, could hear himself stutter with anxiety as he whispered to his fellow associates. All eyes were held fast by the distinct and quick flickering of the gigantic computer.

It was soon time for all the world to know the answer to the question it had for generations sought to have answered clearly.

The contents of this elaborate room with its many sophisticated apparatus, was heavily massed by some fifty scientists, physicists, mathematicians and philosophers from all parts of the world. In each man's mind, they thought in their own particular language, the same thought; would it really work?

Would the giant monster of a machine be able to answer such a previously unanswerable question?

These many intellectuals who had assembled this ultimate computer were now about to witness whether or not all their years of toil would pay off for the human race.

The hush which hovered over the room, now became even more evident, as the teletype arms of the machine began to record its answer to the ultimate question.

The question: How can mankind live on this earth in harmony, without any further wars???

As the letters appeared on the large screen, which magnified their font, the throng of people gathered in the room were struck with awe, as they read...............

1) Thou shalt love the Lord thy God with all thy heart and soul.

2) Thou shalt love thy neighbor as thy self.

3) Thou shalt...

The End

I hope the reader has got the basic idea of what I am attempting to relate. I will now continue by relating a story from my young childhood days at school.

One day in Junior high school, we got into a discussion of the existence of God, with our biology teachers. It was at this time that the teacher gave the most profound explanation of God's existence, that I had ever heard. He produced his wristwatch from his wrist and said. "See this wristwatch? See that it keeps perfect time, seconds, minutes and hours. Now I'm sure you know all the parts it contains, in order to achieve this time keeping function. Well suppose we took it completely apart and tossed all the tiny parts up in the air? Do you think it could come together through evolution or just come about, without the help of an intelligence? Absolutely not. Then how could the universe with all its great wonders, especially man, have just evolved without the existence of an extraordinary intelligence? GOD........

In order to proceed from this point, let me impress upon the reader, the fact that the main ingredient in this whole commentary is faith. God gives us a free will and a complex thinking brain, with which we can use our intelligence, with our common sense to deduce often hidden mysteries. Mysteries are unexplainable facts which we, with our limited brain power, could not comprehend. Remember that one of the most highly rated intellectuals of our time, Albert Einstein, was considered to have used only a minute percentage of his actual brain capacity. So using this logic, how can anyone presume to compare with God's almighty and supreme wisdom? And so it follows, how can we explain His reasons for children dying of hunger, diseases, pestilence, holocausts, etc., etc. So don't tax your limited brain with solving mysteries which the Lord has reserved for Himself. Do however, pursue His words through the Bible and Holy Gospels. There is where God has ordained to reveal Himself through his son, Jesus Christ.

To reinforce some of the previous listed thoughts, in the above paragraphs, let me now include a revelation that came to me one day at Mass.

At a Saturday evening Mass on 1-29-94, while meditating in prayer and listening to a homily relating to a lighted candle, I had the following projected into my thoughts:

Think of a very young child who is completely innocent of everything. Now presume he is your child. You are seated at a table with your child, and on the table between you both is a lit candle. You are now attempting to teach your child that fire is dangerous but also good. You try to explain all the benefits but mainly the hazards of fire. You tell the youngster that he should not put his hand near the flame, because he could get hurt if he did. But, as human nature dictates, his curiosity will overcome his directive and he will eventually attempt to reach out and touch the flame. While watching, you will scold him harshly. After a while when he may persistently try again, you may even hit him more forcibly to punish the disobedience and hopefully keep him from injuring himself at a later date, in your absence. You conclude your lesson and hope you have achieved your goal of teaching the child, since you love him very much. As time passes, curiosity will overpower the child and he will eventually touch the flame. Excruciating pain and possible injury will befall him, as well as sorrow for not having believed his parent, who he knows loves him dearly. You as the parent have done all that you could to ensure your child's welfare, but, have failed and must succumb to human nature with all the heart ache it may entail.

Does that scenario sound familiar to you? What do you conclude from it? Ponder this.

Continuing, let me, if I may, advise the reader, strongly, to read Luke 16, about the rich man and the beggar. It may seem a little harsh but remember how harsh you were when you struck your loving son for not listening to your command. Before I conclude my somewhat lengthy recitation, let me end with an excerpt from one of the Stations of the Cross. The author anonymous writes: Fourteenth Station: My body is put in a tomb: I had no grave of my own. My body was laid in somebody else's tomb. Was it fitting that I be buried in a borrowed tomb? I was always borrowing things. I borrowed a crib in Bethlehem, to be born in. I borrowed Peter's boat to preach from. I borrowed a donkey to ride on when I came into Jerusalem. I borrowed bread and wine to make my body move and my blood flow in history. I borrowed thorns, wood and nails to redeem the universe. Why should my burial be any different? I will go on borrowing things until the end of time, until I have borrowed them all, and make them holy. I will also borrow you. You will be my tongue and my throat, parched. You will be my hands and my feet nailed. You will be my head thronged. You will be my side, lanced. You will be my body stripped. You will be my corpse, buried. And when the borrowing is over, you will be my brothers and my sisters, RISEN!

End of todays session at the keys. Friday 1-23-98.

Session Nine

Well here I finally am again. Back at the key board after at least a year. The time seems to have flown by so quickly and I can hardly remember where I left off. And so I'll try adding a few more lines to this, my biography.

As I said previously, I had lost a whole lot of printed matter in my old computer and now that I've purchased a new one, I feel it is time to continue. I know I went through my father and so I think it would be fitting now to recollect my mother in my earlier years.

My mother was a wonderful and hard working woman. She would leave for work every morning with her sister, my aunt Mickey who lived in the same apartment building as us. They would take an El train each morning to a dress making factory, where they both were fine dressmakers. My mom would leave me to my grandmother, who also had an apartment in the same building. She was another of the loves of my life and I will get to her later.

I can always remember my mother worrying about me. She was always afraid that something bad would happen to me. She never allowed me to own a bike which I desperately wanted, for fear that I would get hit by a car. I remember how I had to sneak my baseball and glove in the garbage so that she wouldn't see them and prevent me from going out to play in the streets.

I remember as a young child how I was so jealous of my two elder sisters who were constantly arrayed in the newest styled dresses, that she would get the patterns for from work. One day I can remember so vividly, although I was maybe four years old, how she felt so bad about my pestering her to make me something too, that she decided to make me a little blue flannel slip. After cladding me in the feminine garment she stood me on our kitchen table where I looked at my reflection from a mirror that was housed within the wall. As I did so I saw the smirks and heard the giggles of my sisters, mom, and grandmother. I began to cry and felt so humiliated that I remember hating them all. I guess that is why today all my female loved ones think I'm a male chauvinist. I guess it stems from then.

Getting back to my mom I know she loved me very much but I was always mad that she babied me so often. As I got older I realized that she had suffered terribly from depression. As a youngster I would always yell at her to snap out of it and think of better things. I could never understand how she couldn't. I used to think to myself "how could she profess to love me and then deny me so much?" It wasn't until I was about thirty years old that I realized what she was going through, because this was when I fell to the dreaded curse of mental depression. That I'll get into later.

Session Ten

Yup! Here I am again. Finally. Its now March.

On our block of 122nd. street, between Pleasant and First Avenue, my friends and I would congregate and participate in all kinds of games, such as stoop ball, stickball, softball, football, Johnny on the Pony and many other things. One of my friend's fathers who was an ex boxer, even made a ring on the sidewalk, and had us all box each other. I can remember my friend's father approaching my father and asking him if he could train me to be a boxer, since he felt I showed potential. I remember my father giving the disappointing answer that " the wife wouldn't go for it". I knew he was right but I can remember the hurt I felt and the hate that he wouldn't stand up to my mother and allow it anyway. Oh well, I guess I should say he went through many hard times with my mother's condition too.

One more thing I'd have to honestly interject at this time relative to my mom is the occasion I had once with a shrink, later in my life. He had asked me if I could remember my mother ever hugging and kissing me. Well, I remained dumb founded. I thought hard and could honestly not remember a time even though I was sure there must have been. The only retort I had to the Doctor was " Gee I can't, and who would remember that?" He immediately replied, "I can." This left me just as dumb founded, but later I would convince myself that it was all because of that cursed depression she suffered from. My father who has passed away already and is happily at peace with God, I'm sure, can relate to the way she suffered and still continues to do so in a nursing home up in Connecticut.

I feel so terribly guilty for not visiting her as often as I should, but like a shrink once convinced me, it would only make the two of us succumb.

And now so I won't forget when I do hopefully get back to my book, let me proceed with my grandmother.

Session Eleven

Yes it's finally me again, after I don't remember how long. Today is Sunday March 19th. 2000, the day before my grandson Anthony Joe's 4th. birthday, and I finally got the writing urge again.

I know I said previously at my last session that I would continue on my beloved grandmother but right now I feel other feelings to write about. It is a time when my wife is on a seven day vacation in Florida with her girl friends and hopefully having a great time. I miss her, but it does seem to inspire my writing urge that she is gone. Don't ask me why. Ha! Ha!

The feelings I have seem as always, to be coming from my dearest and closest friend the Lord Jesus.

Now that I've gratefully reached a ripe young age of 60, I can't help but feel a mellowing out and I am constantly striving to understand more fully God's reason for my existence. I am totally grateful to him for all I've had and have, especially my wife and children and especially my grandchildren.

I'm trying very hard to forgive all who offend me as the Lord has constantly forgiven me. I continually aim to do His will above all and always pray that He might instill in me greater wisdom so that I may live the life He desires of me without so many mistakes and misconceptions. I can most emphatically attest to the fact that my weekly attendance at Mass has not caused me to have a holier attitude but rather has instilled in me a greater hunger to do His will, as hard as I may think it is. I really feel for the people who don't have this same feeling and fervently pray that it will hit them before their demise from this life. Rather then continue to preach I would hopefully suggest that they read Luke 16., as well as the "Stations Of The Cross" which I think I have put to this paper already. In these two writings I feel, is a partial look at the secret of life. That's in my opinion, as lowly as the reader of this text may think it is. I only hope that my family and friends may agree with me and indulge in reading what I suggest. How I feel like a halo is forming around my head so I think I'd better cool it for now. Amen.

Oh! my grandmother. Her name was Vivian, (my daughter Nancy's middle name) Russo. She was a fabulously wonderful woman. She watched me always in my mother's absence which was due to the full time work she did to supplement our fairly poor livelihood. Grandma spoke only Italian and understood much Mitigone. I attribute my slime knowledge of the Italian language to her, and much of my Italian heritage as well.

I can remember so many vivid emotional moments with her. Like how, I must admit, I was a scoundrel, when I snuck into her purse and stole nickels and dimes to promote my occasional flings with the gang. Later in life I felt so bad about this and always hoped and prayed that I would make it up to her. But as life is she had passed away when I was in Okinawa serving as a Marine. My family didn't tell me about it until later when a Company Chaplain informed me of it. It was a time when my eyes did fill with tears of sorrow.

I could remember how my mother always left me a hot breakfast with grandma to serve me after mom had gone to work. I remember hating as I still do, the oatmeal breakfast. I devised a mischievous scheme where I poured a huge amount of salt into the oatmeal pot, while my grandma was unaware, and then when she served it to me I would exclaim, "Look Grandma my mom put too much salt in it!" She would then taste it and after making a disgruntled face, she would scream in Italian words to the effect that "your momma eh pots", and she would consequently throw away all the oat meal and make me whatever I desired, not noticing the smirk of joy that emanated from my face.

The most vivid and loving memory that I still posses is the day that Grandma, Blackie, (our loving dog, a foot high) and I were spending an ordinary afternoon together when low and behold our dog Blackie went mad. He started running throughout the railroad apartment which was our abode. Leaping up on and off all the beds, sofas and such, barking like crazy. Grandma and I could only look at each other with astonishment in our eyes and wonder what could cause the mutt to wrack up. Approximately 10 minutes later in the middle of this fracas, there sounded a knock at our front door. When Grandma and I opened the door we were astonished my the sight of my Uncle Louie. There he was seabag on his shoulder flashing a joyous smile. My grandma hugged and cried with joy as Blackie kept jumping up the full length of my uncle's height, to try and paste a loving lick of a kiss on his jaw. I, who must have been 3 or 4 years old was completely dumbfounded. It is such a loving memory which has been in my subconscious for decades with abundant graditude to our Lord Jesus. Remember we hadn't seen my uncle for approximately 2 years. He had been at war on a destroyer in the U.S. Navy.

As a good friend of mine once phased at a happy time amongst our friendship, "you can't buy this." And so I think I'll head to the spell check now and prepare to print this jive out. See you when God calls me to the keys again. God's peace be with you in the mean time and always as a matter of fact.

Session Twelve

Well look-ie here, I'm back. And it is only a few days ahead, and the Lord has called me to the keys again. It's Saturday morning or I should say Sunday morning at 1:52 A.M. of March 26th. 2000. I couldn't sleep, I guess it was that heavy diner I took my wife to for our 38th. Anniversary yesterday.

I was thinking about my younger years as a growing boy and felt I had to get up and put some of these cherished memories to paper before they would fade into my subconscious again.

I can remember my days on 122nd street between Pleasant Ave. and 1St. Ave. Some of my earliest friends were Marino Stio, Jerry Santarpia,

Frankie Figaroa, Donald, (I forgot) Eddie Menna, (a three time looser) and my most respected friend Joey Nostro. They were mainly my closest friends but there were many more who included the big guys as we called them, like Ralph Salamone, Anthony Stinger, and Nicky Stio, (who is still a close friend to this day). I should also mention my beloved sisters' husbands Ralph and Dom (who gave me my first bike to call my own.) I guess that was to get in good with my loving sister who recently passed away- my Vivian, who I'm sure watches over me from Heaven.

I did all the street things which were so wonderful and hard to describe, like playing all sorts of ball such as foot, base, stick, stoop, hoops, Ringalerio and more. These were among the legitimate games. The bad things need not be recalled. I had a lot of fond memories on this wonderful block but it was in my 15th. year that I really propelled myself into a new and better way of life. It was when I started junior high school at James Otis Junior High School, located in the same building as Benjamin Franklin High School which I later attended as well. It was situated between 116th. and 114th. streets on the East River Drive of East Harlem.

It was there where I first met one of the two of my most beloved friends. Richard Cable is his name. We shared so much in common especially our athletic abilities. He convinced me to join his crew which were called The Bison Jr. Their official abode encompassed the areas of 119th street and Pleasant Ave., and the surrounding blocks. They were a great bunch of guys who really welcomed me. They were all great athletes and participated more totally in all the sports which I previously mentioned. They were strictly an athletic club. I consequently formed many bonds with many new friends from that neighborhood. Again varying in age. The greatest addition which this club imparted on me was the fact that they also had a crew of Bison Jr. DEBS! We at that early age could really sow some oats with these beauties. For you younger readers, debs are girls!!

But honestly the greatest joy I derived from this move, was the fact that I felt free and on my own, since my mother and father who were three and a half blocks away could not scrutinize my every move. I felt even more free as a bird when I later in life went off into the US Marine Corps.

Now I'd like to convey to the reader a little more of the wonderful years I spent in this glorious neighborhood and the many close friends that I acquired there who 'till this day I continue to associate with. But I don't think my writing abilities can do justice to the most loving times I experienced. I did write at one time a poignant story about the old neighborhood which I have on computer and hope to insert at this point to give the reader a small taste of this great place.

I will stop my writing for now in quest of that story so I can see if I can insert it here.

Well here it is, I dug it up.

The Avenue by Joe Gallucci..........

The hour is late, it is dark and oh so very quiet, as your body unwinds, calling for its friendly affiliate, sleep. Suddenly your inner mind seems to bolt from this wonderful twilight feeling just before slumber and commences to take off, as from it's launch pad, like a rocket. Your conscious mind is aghast as it sees its subconscious race through time and space. We decide to board this flight, in hopes of making some semblance of order to it's sightings. Where is it now? Oh!, the old neighborhood. What wondrous memories will it depict on our huge screen before our eyes?

Wow!, there's the Avenue. Why look at the traffic light standing there like a sentinel, guarding the right field, off the alarm fence. And there, just opposite on the northwest corner, is the drug store, with it's illuminations inviting. Over on the southwest corner is that place of numerous unforgettable good times, the "Night-Hawks" club. Now we cross to the other side and find ourselves at the southeast section of

47

this intersecting street. Here we can see that wonderful lamppost, which bore the name of this fabulous place. Coupled to this fine edifice is our memorable alarm. Just across from this dynamite duo, stood a red brick building, which at it's corner point was housed a mirror. This mirror would reflect its numerous passers-by, like the Avenue's inner soul. It was also a convenient place for the "Cole" to take a double check.

We turn this mirrored corner and proceed down the block. That wondrous block which was the dwelling of a fraction of the many fine people who inhabited this loving neighborhood. Proceeding down this block we first come upon Fred and Dolly's quaint daytime diner, where many a malt and such were devoured. Just ahead that building, with the fine stoop, which enabled many an exiting stoop ball game, to be played. Further on as we pass the many apartment houses and the old public school which encompassed a third of the opposite side of the street, we would finally come to that wondrous place, known affectionately, as our park. Who could forget the marvels this fine area held for us. The tight and extremely competitive basketball games, which we had, and/or the many romantic episodes which our tough sides would practice, on one of it's famous benches.

Crossing the East River Drive, or safely traversing it via the overpass, would bring us to our famous watering hole, where on a hot summer day many a fine lad could be seen bathing in the dank, filthy but refreshing waters of the East River. The more brazen would be captured as they dove from the high overhanging overpass or swimming to the other side, to land on Randalls Island.

Back on the avenue, one could recall so many other aspects of the neighborhood. The many fascinating stickball games which were so much a part of our culture. And what about "Cuschas", where one could still smell the aroma of her tempting foods and baked goods, as they flowed from the greasy kitchen...and the only place you could see the raisins walk off of her buns. The shoe maker and liquor store. Scotti's and Charlie Ding Ding's candy stores. And not to forget the parties at one of the Bison Deb's houses. Boy how these places and events conjure up memories.

Names, especially, nicknames, were so prevalent. Monikers like Moe, McGraw, Cole, Rags, Do-Do, Ju-Ju, Cap, Pickels, Head, Rabbit, Greek, Butter Fly, Prunes, Muse, Smash, Frog Eyes, Baboink, Hoot, Punchy Marsh Moon, Beals are just a few of many. The comradeship which these nicknames seem to foster were like the comradeship shared by Jesus and his Apostles, and as is the Espirt de Corps, in the modern day Marine Corps.

It would be impossible for a single soul to capture, correctly what so many have lived. Hopefully this narrative will act as a catalyst for your own memories.

SEE YOU ON THE AVENUE!

Session Thirteen

Here I am again, it is Sunday morning of April 2nd. 2000, and since the clocks were pushed a hour ahead it is 4:32 am. I can't sleep and my mind is just racing with new things to write.

When I last left off, I said I would dig up an old story I had wrote relative to my beloved old neighborhood. Well I did, and rather than typing it all over again I decided to just add it as pages 19, 20, and 21 of this my writings. And now on to another subject.

While trying to sleep tonight I kept thinking that one of the criterias of my writing was to leave some sort of a legacy to my loved ones. My children and especially my grand children.

And above all to the youngest and most beloved, that being Anthony Joe who I love him so. I will address my thoughts to Anthony Joe, but do wish them for all to try to adhere to.

First of all grandpa, always remember that all you have and ever will achieve through out your life, is a special gift from God. Always remember that, and live your life accordingly. Show God our Father heartfelt love and devotion always, because He will always be with you, protecting you and loving you. Always trust in him and never allow the masses of society, the media or the boob tube to sway you from your trust in him. He loves you even more than I do, which does sound impossible I'm sure. Strive in life to learn as much as you could. Always be an avid reader. Read any subject you like at first and later when you have mastered reading your world can be opened to all the wonders in Gods Universe. Later when you are guided by higher learning principals you will see how great the advantage of being a good reader was. Always remember that you are never too old to learn something new.

I throughout my life have learned this through, ordinary life experiences. And since I am now in my 60th year of Gods precious gift of life, I feel I have some credentials to speak with. I know my own children look on me at times as just an old codger who is out of touch and antique in my ways. I don't blame them for this since I felt the same about my parents. But remember there is only one Being who can love you more than your parents and that is the One I'm sure you know. So always listen to the advice of your parents.

Having been brought up in the Catholic faith has taught me a lot of things. To elaborate a bit let me start by saying. When I retired from the Sanitation department after working for 20 years, My mind was opened up drastically. I now found the time to devote to other matters such as reading and learning other things like computers and such. I once read a book whom a fellow worker had recommended. It was called

"Self Hypnotism", and it was one of the most enlightening books I've ever read. In fact it was so impressive that I gave it to all my family that Christmas as a gift.

In this book among other things relative to the human mind, I learned that the subconscious within us is one of the most powerful gifts God has bestowed on us. This is not in the book but, I 've come to my own conclusion that it is really the Holy Spirit within us. The book states that your subconscious is more powerful than any computer ever devised. It has the power to remember every thought, sight, smell or words you've every herd. This goes as far back as your original conception. Its main function is to protect you at all costs. It will punish you if you do wrong and will make you aware of any dangers. It will also hide from you things that it feels may hurt you. There were many other concepts I learned from this book and with the help of God I've put a lot of them to good use as they pertain to God. Many a time I've tried to tell all my children to always think positive and have faith that God will always provide for you. Don't get negative and say such things as "oh! I give up" or "I CAN'T". That particular phrase was constantly eradicated from my mind in the Marine Corps. These negative phrases are taken literally by your sub conscious. Like when you say "Oh! that person gives me a headache". Your subconscious hears and says okay you want a head ache, I'll give you one. And low and behold you got it. Or " I'm getting a cold" etc.

Every body through out life goes threw tribulations but never as much as our savior did, and He Triumphed, as he instills you to do.

Take care of yourself naturally but don't ever thrive on thinking negatively or hopelessly. Trust in Jesus and don't worry about your health. If God wants you there is nothing that can prevent you from going to Him. If you maintain this outlook on life you will find it more rewarding.

I've recently viewed a Doctor of philosophy and such on channel 13. I taped his seminar and was astounded to find that his teachings coincided tremendously with my own. His name is Dr. Wayne Dyer and the tape number is 291b. If any of you get the chance please request it from the president of my video collection, Amanda Gallucci.

Well its 5:30 am now and I think I'll hit the sack. see ya next time, If God wants. Theresa just arrived home so I think I'll have a good sleep now. Goodnight.

Session Fourteen

I'm back now again, sooner than I expected. I was in the club this afternoon at about 4p.m. and I had about an hour to kill before I go to church. Which I normally do on Saturday afternoon at the 5:30 Mass at O.L.A., my parish church.

While watching the Yankee game which was on TV. I got the urge to write about my favorite hang out, which is that where I was, my friendly club. I thought of writing the piece strictly for the club but later felt that it would be a fine addition to my bio. And so now I will try to describe to the reader one of my life long loves. our club. From this point I will copy from the hand written notes I compiled this afternoon at the club.

The year is 2000. the price of a pack of cigarettes has gone from its original price of 25 cents a pack in the 1950's to a total of $4'50 a pack. Technology has forged ahead as quickly as the prices of ordinary essentials. The only consistency being the change.

Through it all one could still find a place where you could get a top notched meal with a lot of genuine camaraderie for a measly $10.00.

The address of 3194 on Westchester Ave. in the Bronx, is the place where you'll find the white door with the prominent affixed sign of members only, on its face. It is the Italian American Club which had its roots in the same building for decades previous. Its membership over the years has changed mainly by attrition of its older members due to death.

Presently the breed of members which inhabit the rolls of membership to this club are unique in the fact that the majority of them have all migrated from a fantastic place known as PLEASANT AVE. It was there where some of the most closest and oldest bonds were formed. The Bison culture came to the old Italio-American club. The group of friends ranging from childhood on the corner to the average age of 60 years can be seen regularly on a Wednesday night devouring delicious meals and imbibing as well.

The normal attendance of members consists of guys who live, in Jersey, Long Island, Manhattan and up state, to name a few places. Anywhere from 15 to 30 guys is the norm for a meal. No wonder Our Cooks are so temperamental. Our wives who are glad not to participate are relieved of cooking duty for that night.

We have at least four formidable cooks being short one great one who is away on vacation, it is defiantly hard for them and they deserve much credit and thanks for these great nights. The satisfaction of all is hard to accomplish, but well worth the effort.

"You can't buy this" As George Comoutsos would say. Birthdays of each member are cordially celebrated with large decorative Birthday cakes containing beautifully lit colored candles and a melodious chorus of guys singing happy birthday to the year older coump. The end of the song is incredibly sung in a high and mighty pitch by our very own Charlie Irish. His vocal rendition on "to you" is synonymous with another year of life to thank God for.

Much pasta and such is consumed by the crew each Wednesday night. especially adhering to this standard are guys like Dennis, and Richie Calbi who are our pasta devouring kings.

The characters and conversations which emanate from this true to life place would make conventional movie and TV. portrayals seem bland and artificial.

Some of the new members have been brought from the dead, so to speak, from our annual father and son stickball game, which was originated by one of our members wife. Mikey and Flo Lentini. It is a grand day which occurs every September and has gone on for the last 13 years. Old neighborhood people gather to play stickball with their grown sons. It gives the kids a taste of what life was like for their parents on the streets of Harlem. Wives and daughters attend as well and all have a grand time playing or watching. Lunch and drinks are provided to all. In each succeeding year the crowd of players and onlookers has grown tremendously. People from as far as Florida and Oklahoma have attended. This past year of 1999 saw the first publicity bombardment that we've had. Articles in the NY Times and Daily News were prevalent as well has TV. coverage on a few NY channels. Why we were also featured on a world wide net page. And so you can see how we've been able to muster even more candidates to our weekly get together.

Besides the people we've incorporated from this stickball session we have also welcomed a few guys back from the proverbial can. Such friends have provided us with deeper and funnier insights to the life inside, and we have provided them with heartfelt love and forgiveness as I'm sure is Gods will.

Besides the friendly banter that reverberates from the clubs mirrored walls there is always the friendly games of poker, pinnacle and especially conti card games which constantly lighten or full the participants pockets.

The washer woman who definitely permeate the gathering are the only disparaging words I would add. But all considered it is a place of love and friendship, and I pray God to watch over us all. Hopefully God will let us meet some day with all our dearly departed friends, like Sonny Mc graw, Flappy, Lonnie, to mention a few of the most recent among many. I had once built a fake tomb stone which listed all of them, but it didn't sit too well with the majority, so I'll just pray for them in my own personal way.

Hoping this narrative does not offend any one, I'll sign off now Praying that God will continue to love and protect us all, even you Ant.(F.S.).

God's Peace be with you,

Pal,

Joey G.

And now before I close for the night and retire, let me list a few subjects which I'd like to include in some future sittings at the keys. They are the three occasions in my life when I felt close to death. Also to mention some real close friends. An don't forget to mention your bouts with depression. I think I wrote of them previously but I also think it was among all the text that I had previously mentioned had inadvertently erased from my computers memory. Now don't forget. Too tired now to continue. See you when I get back. Sunday morning 4/9/2000 at 2:30 AM. nightly night

Session Fifteen

Here I am back again, today being Monday morning at 12:17 am of the 1st. of May 2000.

In the previous paragraph I mentioned that I would devote some space to explaining my bouts of depression. On further considerations I've decided not to since it is, something I hate to even recount. The phycitrists today have realized that talk therapy is not as beneficial as proper medication is. And so I've decided to eliminate that part of my life story since it is such a dreaded part. I can only accept it as God's will and I'm sure He has instilled a lot of wisdom in me for having gone through it. Actually if a scrink was to read this I'm sure he would have tons of traumatic explanations for my behavior anyway, even if it were Dr. Melfi. So lets just let it lay. Only remember that if any of the readers ever feel, they are encountering any prolonged symptoms of depression, they must definitely seek help. This will definitely rectify the ill feelings. Enough on that.

And now for three distinctive occasions in my life when I felt as though I would loose my life. Each of these true happenings did teach me a profound lesson in life.

The first I will account is when I was probably 11 or 12 years of age. I participated in various athletic endeavors as a member of the 'Boys Club Of New York' One of these was the use of the huge swimming pool. One day after practicing to swim the short distance of the width of the pool, which was I'd guess at some 30 to 40 feet in length. I decided I was then proficient enough as a swimmer to now attempt the same swim but only at the deeper end of the pool, which was 9 to 10 feet deep. Oh, incidentally I neglected to add that my previous practice attempts were in a depth of only 3 feet. I made the swim back and forth 4 laps. I was never able to swim before this.

When my nerve was up I briskly walked to the deep end of the pool and dived in. I started out fine, but as I reached the center of the pool, I just got panicky and began to sink. A fellow club member who was swimming near by, spotted me and came to my rescue, as he thought. But as he got near to me I quickly folded me two arms completely around him in a vise grip bear hug. This caused us both to quickly reach the bottom of the pool, struggling with each other. It was at this point that the elderly big lifeguard on duty finally appeared and pulled me safely up to the surface. My friend scurrying away like a minno from a shark.

After some minutes of expectorating a huge amount of water from my lungs, I felt fine. And after a while went back to the 3 feet and swam back and forth a few more times. Proud of myself for the rest of my life, was the thing I did next. I walked right up to the 9 feet section of the pool and proceeded swim back and forth like a newly hatched fish.

Thank you Lord, for making me see that fear is only mind over matter.

A second life threatening event happened a little later in life when I was about 16 years old. My friends and I had a little spot of grass which ran adjacent to the East River Drive from 122nd. to 123rd. streets in East Harlem. On this formidable patch of grass we would often assemble for some rough full tackle football games, minus the equipment which is so prevalent to youngsters today.

At this particular time the city was refurbishing an entranceway leading up onto the Willis Ave. bridge. There were a few large holes dug as big as bomb craters and they had long thin steel poles protruding up from out of them. I guess for reinforcing of the concrete that would later be poured into the holes, for foundations.

Well on this particular day I was playing end for our team. The play in the huddle called for me to go out to the right and long, for a pass. On the snap of the ball I charged out as fast as I could and 2 seconds later turned to the quarterback, who had already planted the ball right in my arms. I turned immediately and began to take one step in the direction of the goal and as I did I saw that I was directly over one of the holes I previously described, and my whole life must have flashed before me, when all of a sudden from my left side appeared one of my lifelong friends, Mikey Lentini, who hit me with a perfect leg tackle which knocked me completely to the left onto the beautiful green grass, alive and well and thankful.

The lesson for me there was to listen a little harder to my moms constant scolding of being careful in the streets.

My next close encounter was not really life threatening but really life instructive.

We were on a night patrol one night in the bushes of Okinawa. I can remember that I couldn't see my hand in front of my face, because I literally tried doing it. Our platoon leader had advised us that it was strictly a reckon patrol. meaning no firing, was to be done. Only to see if you spot any enemy, (in this case actual marines dressed in enemy uniforms), and to then report back with numbers and location. We started out with one guy being the point first about ten yards ahead of us. Then I came and a few others behind me in graduating distances a part. After walking for about 10 minutes out with our rifles loaded with blanks, (thank God), I herd 'stop who goes there', a second later the point guy comes and goes running by me in the dark. Me like a jerk assume the position of John Wayne and from the hip fire off my entire clip of eight rounds from my M1. All I saw was blind white light and the loud pop, pop of the 8 rounds directed at the sound of the voice. With my clip extinguished I proceeded to high tail it back with my fellow

Marines. As I caught up to the point guy who had passed me earlier, he proceeded to turn and fire his M1, point blank into my stomach. All I could see was a red and white flash which blinded me momentarily. I felt the hot paper which capped off the gun powder and replaced an actual shell-head, spray all over my face. Not to mention the ringing in my ears which I had for about an hour.

Boy did I learn a lesson that night. It was one of many from my many days of living and training in the fields. I would never disobey an order again.

Enough for tonight, see you next time.

Session Sixteen

Continuing, I hope the reader is well updated on the writers inner self. And so I will proceed with the story. As we left off Joe, had just finished breakfast and made a bee line to his computer. There he hoped to recapture his vivid dream from the previous night. He was a little hesitant because he knew the dream entailed him speaking with Jesus Christ. The reason he was so reluctant was because he knew no one could compare to Jesus's wisdom. And so to convince himself that God would understand, he proceeded to write down the exact words he had uttered and those which he had heard. Joe realized that God had communicated many times over the centuries, in dreams to various people. Mary, Joseph and Mosses to name a few. So still with trepidation he continued. Going along with this reasoning he began to convince himself that he would go on. This he proceeded to do.

Joe's eyes opened to a radiant bright light. He was astounded by the fact that his eyes were completely adjusted to its brilliance, and not at all discomforting. A most UN mistakable Image of Jesus Christ appeared before him. From his beautiful face which housed His whiskered covered lips, He said; "Hello Joe". I was dumbfounded and immediately went to my knees, closed my eyes and uttered, "My Lord and my God". He then said to me, "Arise My son, and sit with me at table, be freshed with some bread and wine".

He and I proceeded to a nearby table of beautiful cherry wood construction. One I knew my son inlaw, carpenter would deeply appreciate. Upon the elaborate table was a rounddish carved wooden jug. From the odor which emanated from the open jug, I presumed it contained a delicious wine. The bread which lay beside the jug was throwing off its own aroma of just baked bread.

As we began to enjoy the bread and wine, He nonchalantly asked me a question. He began with, "my son," then went on to ask. "Why do you question so often, Our Fathers reasoning, even though you admit to, not having an iota of intelligence compared to the Lord our God". I then hesitantly answered. "Lord, If I may, I'd like to just say that I don't know why, God doesn't send an ordinary person to earth. One who possessed infinite powers, such as was Yourself, Lord? But this time make him accessible to all peoples of the world, to preach Your word. But to emphasis the point, make him show them through examples and miracles.

"What with the new technological advances, You have granted us, such as TV, radio and most recently the world wide Internet, etc. This could be accomplished, I am sure." I was almost out of breath while I steadied myself to receive

His answer. Again, "My son, how often has Our Father sent people through out history who were ignored, Myself included. Recall one of Luke's Gospels had told it vividly, how the poor beggar man sat outside the home of the rich man and his brothers. The dogs would lick his sores on his body when they had finished the scraps that were thrown to them." I Fearfully interrupted Him here by stating. "Yes My Lord I recall, How Abraham exclaims the rich man that even if one came from the dead, they would not believe." "Oh my son, I'm glad you've remembered that one. So what makes you think it would work, your way?" After a short time of contemplation and or hesitation, I retorted with. "Lord isn't it worth a try, even if it converts just one person?" With this reply I began to fear my forwardness may have got me in trouble with the Lord. But, contrary to my ill feelings, the Lord replied with his normal melodious tone of "My son, you make a good point, as Job. You have an e (for effort), will be granted your wish as at Sohdem and Gamora".

At this point I was really trembling with fear and exclaimed emphatically, "Oh Lord please not I. Let it be someone more deserving of Your love." It was at this precise moment that a streak of early morning sunlight snuck through a defective venetian blind, in my window and placed itself squarely in both my eyes. I blinked and awoke immediately. I felt refreshed, after a hardy yawn I was ready for another day. The dream from the following night was just a memory for now.

I proceeded to perform my normal morning activities. After relieving myself at camode, I proceeded to wash my face and hands. When I looked into the mirror I noticed that I had a three day growth on my face and looked like a ware wolf. Since I had to go to the bank this day I figured I'd better shave, before I get mistaken for a bank robber.

As I shaved, While gazing at my face in the mirror, to my front. I noticed a gleam in my eyes, which I had never noticed before. It was like a sunset, kissing the waves on an ocean. I know I had seen this look somewhere but just couldn't think of where or when. Contemplating this made my dream come back. And oh, there it was in the eyes of my Lord. This to me seemed impossible, but to the contrary was exactly what I saw. I took a deep breath, trying to relax myself. Looking more fervently at my reflection off the mirror I noticed an even more mysterious fact. The birthmark or skin growth that I possessed on the left side of my face, just below my sideburn, had completely disappeared. O my God what is happening to me? I shut my eyes and reverently began to pray. In hopes that if this is what I was thinking, was true, then I would need much guidance from Him. My Lord.

To convince myself that this was not just a figment of my imagination, I proceeded to try some magical things. The first thing I did was to try to project my mind into that of my wife's. And low and behold, I was not only in her mind, but a vivid image of her was in my thoughts as well. She was conversing with a fellow worker and in her mind she was thinking, "Gee, I hope this girl can follow the directions I gave her, properly". This phenomena really scared me but I would have to test it further. I picked up the daily newspaper which my wife had left on the kitchen table, before she went to work. Thinking this would be a great test, I proceeded to write down numbers. The numbers I wrote were all of the numbers that came out, the previous day in the N.Y. state Lotteries. Hastily writing on a plain paper pad. I inscribed all various type numbers that may have been drawn yesterday. The list consisted of the 'Lotto 59', 'Take 5' the 'Pick 10' and mid day and evening 'Pick 3' and 'Pick 4' numbers. I even threw in numbers of winning horses that I was sure were in the papers too.

To my unimaginable surprise I was completely shocked to see that, I had correctly listed every single number that had been drawn, even the coinciding horses to their number. This really put me in a state of euphoria, and I then sat down in hopes of meditating and trying to comprehend what was happening to me.

Now that was the past that I fooled with, what would it be like to predict the future outcomes. So out of my revere, I continued to write down on a fresh paper, the numbers I foresaw for the present day, which were yet to be drawn. I would check tomorrow morning when the daily newspaper arrived.

In the mean time I would try various feats to convince myself that I was in deed the bearer of some wonderful phenomena.

Approaching my window, I noticed a pigeon, who was perched on a flower pot my wife had affixed to the sill. I opened the window and to my utter surprise the pigeon did not fly away. Even more astonishingly, he looked up at me and said. Yes, I said, he said to me, "Hi Joe, got some crumbs for the old bird?" What can I say, but I was terrified, and immediately pulled down the window and ran to my favorite spot of comfort. My bed.

For hours I laid there, with visions of all the fantastic things I could do with my new found capabilities. But wait a minute. That ever present dream, flashed before my eyes and I was quickly attuned to what had transpired in it. Was this Jesus's fulfillment of the query I had imposed on Him? Oh! God, yes it was. I was completely convinced of the afro mentioned statement and diverted my thoughts to strictly that.

What I recall having said was, "why can't an ordinary person have the infinite power to explain to the world, through miraculous acts of God's Will. I think that was the essence of what I had suggested.

Well, your an ordinary Joe. Lets see if you can carry the ball for the Man.

Okay, Joe said, "I will try to fulfill my theory". Joe firstly began to deeply meditate and while meditating decided to speak with the Lord.

Dear Lord please, please grant me the wisdom and courage to accomplish my prescribed task. Let me not be contrary to any of Your teachings, and most of all please do not let me ever loose my faith, love and gratitude for You. In my quest which I have so belligerently, chose to undertake, please forgive me if I am wrong and help me with wisdom to comprehend and accept Your will. I will truly admonish any monetary and or material gains on my own behalf. But truly strive to accomplish your will only. With this most fervent prayer, I do take upon the task I have proclaimed to You in my dream.

That night when Joe's wife Annette, prepared and served him his dinner, he did not even enlighten her about this capabilities or plans. When she complained of a headache and pains in her arthritic neck, he did attempt to ease her pains and eliminate them completely. This he did by simply suggesting same in his mind, with complete confidence for attainment. His wife became immediately chipper and proclaimed in a happy tone that she felt so much better all of a sudden. Joe remarked that, "it might be those motrem pills you took a little while ago." She retorted with, "boy it took them long enough to kick in". Continuing, she said "how about us going to a movie". I erroneously exclaimed that I had saw almost everything and was feeling a little down, myself tonight. She astounded me by saying "Okay, lets stay home and I'll give you a rub down." This to me was great news, for I knew we would eventually make like a beast with two backs and then fall gracefully to sleep. I could use a rest from the constant rederick which churned in my mind. I would rest tonight and hopefully be refreshed in the morning to proceed to analyze my situation and plan the future of my task.

Session Seventeen

As I had predicted the evening and night came to pass. The next morning after my usual formalities, including a kiss for my wife as she departed the house for work, I immediately reached for the newspaper and without even a doubt, confirmed all my previous days lottery picks to be correct.

Okay that's it, now for some deep and serious planning.

On the next day, which happened to be a wonderfully cool and clear day. The day which all my friends did look forward to. For it was the evening of that same day that we all met, ate a great meal, (prepared by Popcorn), had our garrulous and gesticulating conversations, and played poker afterwards.

On this particular Wednesday evening it was the Birthday of Cap. This called for our customary birthday celebration, which consisted of Charlie Irish's fantastic rendition of happy birthday after we concluded our meal of pasil lentil and roast pork with all the trimmings. This was a tradition we carried out for years. I had posted a list on our bulletin board with all the names and accompanying birth dates. Mine was just after Cap's on the 27th., and I looked forward to the coming Friday, which would be my turn. Everyone would shake the birthday persons hand, wish him the best and more than likely kiss the guy who became a year older.

To get a little flavor of the club and the guys, I would now like to express a few stories, If I may.

First let me state that the age bracket of most of the guys who attend is from 50 to 80 years of age. Now you must realize that all were brought up in the streets of East Harlem. We have all of the hang ups and fine qualities that only Harlemites would appreciate. We were friends from childhood, and remained together since. Many a new attendee who might have been a friend of one of the regulars, often said that, they never saw anyone else who had this many friends who stood together for so many years. As our man Gorge Comoutsaos coined our motto phrase, "You can't buy this". It is certainly true, and a motto we've adopted.

After coffee and cake, the pinochle players would head off to a cleaned table, for their $5. a man game, to be wagered on a number, in hopes of a bigger windfall of money. The poker players would mosey on into the back room, where the oversized, green covered table awaited. The first 9 players would begin the game, while others would wait in the wings for a seat to be vacated. There would still be guys who just sat around and bullshitted and imbibed what liquor was available. Louie wooden leg would usually host this friendly group. Television was rare and usually when a major sport event was being televised.

The language was normal street language, with the word F*** being the main expletive used. As I had mentioned in my small biography, I can't say that word, not even write it. Ha! Ha! You may wonder how I could survive in such an atmosphere. But hey, I did 3 years in the U.S.M.C. and never used it there either. I remember once my older sister, Marion had told me, "brother, the only people that have to use that word, are those who hope to show themselves as tough." That advice stood with me always as my love for her has. Thank God I never had to use it to show toughness. My actions would be more talkative in that respect.

Anyway getting back to the club, the guys would joke and tell stories of when we were kids or talk about upcoming events, such as our annual Father and son stickball game. The event was the brain child of my friend Mickey Lentini's wife Florinda. But the work became Mikey's burden.

Speaking now of a couple of fun guys, one could not go any further than to mention Charlie Irish and George Comotsos. These two individuals would be the preverbal clowns of our crew. Charlie being the more physical type and Georgi being the funny ad-libbing type.

Charlie would often remove both bridges of his teeth, and project his funny stories in a toothless fashion. George was more of a Don Wrickels type, with a sprinkling of Robin Williams. Both of them are hilarious and I'm sure could have made it in show business, if so inclined.

Among this assortment of varied personalities were a few ex-cons, who had done their bids to society and were warmly accepted by us all. To mention just two, let me say first, that their names will be changed to protect the innocent. Ha! Ha! First there is Willy rags who spent the majority of his life in college, as he calls it. And let me say that it is not so untrue, because there are plenty of college graduates who haven't got an iota of his common sense. He is a nice looking guy, with bluish eyes and a slightly bald head. He is a true harlemite and often boasts "there is nobody that can compare to a harlemite.

Willy Rags can tell stories on end about college and Harlem. He is a great guy though. I knew him from the time I first went 119th. street. We were on the same 100 lbs. Boys Club basketball team and naturally the ever famous Bisons. The Bisons was the fabulous crew of people from Pleasant Avenue. I say people because we also had girls. We had the bison Deb crews as well, which coincided with the Bison's, Srs., Jrs. and Midgets. Many of these individuals were intertwined for life in marriage.

Getting back to Willy Rags, he was the type of guy that would do anything for a friend. And he has a heart of gold. I never met a guy with more balls then him.

And now for just a second ex collegiate, there is the big R. RR, had a million stories pertaining to his college career and was very funny. In order to supplement his supply of jokes, I would often bring him new material which I got off the Internet.

Now for a few more regular guys. At this point I would be very much a miss if I didn't mention my two favorite friends. They are the only two guys that wear a Crucifix ring on their finger as well as myself. I guess we are not macho enough to not flaunt our love for God.

Richie is a guy with a heart of gold who is always reliable, a hard worker, who just recently retired. This he did some 18 years after my retirement. Richie would have been my best man when I got married, but he was away in the Army, when I did marry. It was Libby who I hung out with very much just before I got married, who filled in Richies slot. Libby who Baptized my first son Joey, did not remain on this earth for too long, since he was killed by a bullet. This we won't go into since it still hurts to have lost him.

Continuing With Rich, as I think I did previously mention, was the guy I first met from the Bisons. He introduced me to all the other guys, who I befriended when I was 13 years old. Richie to me has all the qualities of a rock solid friend. His brother Dennis is just as special. I nicked named Dennis 'Scawla Macaroon', since he is the one who dumps all the macaroni from the scalding pot, for Popcorn the cook, on Wednesday and Friday evenings. I got to know Dennis very well in the last few years and can honestly say he is a clone of his brother Richie, especially heart wise.

Now to my ever favorite friend. He will be the one that I entrust to be the first to read this my hopeful attempt at writing. There is no other person on earth that I feel such love for, other than my wife and children, and especially my grand children. I always look on Peter as 'Saint Peter'. He has helped me in so many ways in the few decades that I've known him. He was especially helpful to me in my depression stages.

In the past year he had major heart surgery and while in the hospital lost his wife to our Lord. I prayed and thank the Lord for his eventual rehabilitation. He once told me he would want me to eulogize him at death. But, I said I would not be able to.

He is great in every aspect and is not ashamed to praise the Lord, as quite a few of my friends seem not to do. His only downfall in my estimation is the fact that he is ULTRA sensitive. One of our greatest friends, Flappy who passed away a few years ago, used to joke that he once went to a football game with Pete, and when the quarter back huddled with his teammates, Peter would ask Flappy if they were talking about him. How's that Ro?

There are so many other guys to mention, but the length of this thing could go on for ever. So I hope all the guys won't scold me for not giving a little about each of them. I'll just mention their first names and wish them all my love.

And now for some monikers........ Cap, Cole, Flappy, Mc Graw, Beals, Greek, Rags, Moon, <Marsh, Gaboink, Head, Frog eyes, Hoot, Bo-Bo, Popcorn, Scawla Macoroon, G-G, Moe, Nuts, Punchy, Prunes, Wee Gee, Etc. Etc.

Yes I did mention even the ones who have departed this life, for I'm sure we will see them all again in the after life. Those are only some of the nick names, there is also plenty with common names such as Joe, etc.

Well by now I presume the reader has gotten a fine taste of the characters I had decided to try my talents on first. If I could convince and convert those the ones I loved, I would think it would be a convincing thing to spur me on to the world.

Session Eighteen

I arrived at the club on this particular Wednesday at approximately 4 P.M. I greeted all the guys present with customary hello greetings. I then proceeded to the coffee machine housed in the kitchen, and poured myself a cup of coffee.

As I was pouring my coffee into the Styrofoam cup, (which I was known to often accidentally spill on the floor or persons,) I noticed my pal Charlie Irish standing adjacent to me at the counter, applying his normal 8 teaspoons of sugar to his coffee. This was a practice that Charlie followed every time he had a cup of coffee. All us guys would often comment in no uncertain terms, that he was nuts using so much sugar and that he was hyper because of it. These comments would automatically trigger his LOUD response of "BUT I'M NOT HYPER". This reply would set us all off in laughter.

So there I was, with my plan for tonight all prepared, when I thought to myself. Lets eliminate Charlies over anxious desire for so much sugar. I decided to rid him of the urge for sugar completely and harmlessly. This I did, without ever letting on to him or anyone in the room that I did. Simply putting my hand on his left shoulder in a friendly jester of hello, I imposed the spell on him in my thoughts.

The scene that transpired at this juncture was really hilarious. Charlie took his first sip of the hot brewed coffee and all of a sudden spit the whole thing out, like a child who hated the medicine his mom administered. He then proclaimed that it tasted horrible and that he would never add sugar again. All in attendance laughed histerically as Charlie proceeded to empty his cup in the sink and poured a new cup, without sugar. After tasting it a second time, the sugarless coffee was heartily devoured. This action on his part triggered off another course of laughs, from all, especially yours truly.

The late afternoon continued to go bye with all the normal pinnocle games and conti. Conti being the popular game played daily, which provided the house to make money from the cut of the game, which went for the clubs upkeep.

I myself sat at a table and played pinnocle, with my partner Billy, and our adversaries, Popcorn and Patty.

We all broke up at approximately 5:45, when Popcorn retreated to the kitchen where he had slaved all day, preparing the fine meal for tonight. Donning his red cooks apron, he yelled out for Dennis, ("Scawala Macaroon") to accompany him.

It was then that all the hungry awaiting members started to assemble near their tables, trying to get served before that table one crew. Which I myself was an occupant of.

Everyone would form a line which focused on the pot which Dennis had recently deposited the normal 10 to 12 pounds of pasta into. Popcorn would then administer the sauce to same and henceforth distribute to the awaiting bowels as they passed his way.

After we had eaten our main course, we would have our coffee and cake. Regular cake if a birthday celebration was not in order. Regular friendly banter would always permeate this occurrence.

It was now that I decided to try out my rehearsed plan.

"Excuse me", I said, "I have something very important to say, and I hope you all will give me your undivided attention". Noticing all 30 of the diners in front of me, I visualized myself in their place and wondered if they were thinking "au Oh, what has this nut got to say", and things of that nature. But wait I could if I wanted to actually read their minds. But not now, I had to stay focused. Going on, (after all the derision's were complete), I continued with " I have a real unbelievable thing to tell you all". The room seemed to have quieted a bit, so I took the ball and ran. "This thing that happened to me a few days ago is known only by my wife and I". More silence, more yardage. "Let me first start by saying a similar thing happened to Jesus Christ", then the expected jokes relative to religion ensued. I quickly quelled the few obnoxious interrupters and proceeded with. "Exactly what I was trying to say is what happened to Jesus by the people he congregated with. They were amongst the most avid decanters of his power. Why, I can't explain, but I truly hope that you, all my loving friends will not treat me as badly." Again after all the cracks, I continued with, "I can do anything, yes, I mean anything." Oh boy did the ball breaking and laughter commence now. After tons of stupid questions I lied and said, "I can only do things for good, by that I mean lets say one of you has terminal cancer, yes, I can cure you permanently, here and now.

Of that or any other ailment". Just as I was about to continue I heard the voice of Mikey, who even though he was at the furthest part of the room, I could hear him like he was using a microphone. He was always a loud talker and we often said he was brought up in a saw mill. His Question was, "why don't you pick the winning Lottery numbers for us, like you and your computer were never able to do for us before".

He was referring to the Lottery pool I had established. When every Wednesday night with the help of "Scawla Macaroon", we'd collect 5 dollars a man and I would figure the hot and due numbers in the up coming Lotto 59 game in N.Y., and then wheel them. In about 3 years of this we came real close only once. We had six of the total seven numbers drawn on one game panel, that including the supplementary number. We missed just one number which I didn't include in the numbers wheeled. And that number was 43. I was devastated because I had wanted to play it just for the fact that it was my wife's birth year, but it wasn't coming up as a strong number, so I eliminated it. I had wheeled just 20 numbers for a total of about 100 games. We did manage to have 1 ticket with 5 of the main six drawn. It paid around $1,300. We also caught ten tickets with four numbers, which paid $68.00 each. And I think 4 tickets with 3 and the supplementary number for about $14.00 each. I forgot the grand total but I gave each of about 25 guys $105., and still had about $300. in our pool. Oh! well this coming winter, We'll do better.

Now that you know what Mikey was referring to, I'll continue.

Diligently I proceeded to try to explain how I had the dream. And what transpired when I awoke. My words seemed to just bounce off the walls as the chatter and banterous catcalls persisted.

I decided to work some miracles there and then. With a harsh loud voice I approached Cap, who was one of the strongest antagonists and a very weak religious orientated, good friend.

I happened to know as all else of our closest friends did, that Cap was physically ill, and had a steel plate in his head. The plate was inserted in an earlier bout with death.

"All right wise guy", I bellowed. Putting my right hand on his head. "You are now completely cured of all your disabilitating ailments." All of a sudden he sprang from is chair as if shot from a cannon. Shouting at the top of his lungs. "He did it, he did it. This numbness did it." All the eyes in the room were focused on him in disbelief. Some even accused him of being in cahoots with me to cajole them.

The next thing I established was the fact that I knew that there would be doubting Thomas's in abundance. So now I would convince each and every one of them. I would advance on all of them individually and cure each of them of any malady which they may have possessed. I also stated that for time sake I would only grant one to all. I explained that, they could use their prescribed miracle or spell as they had proclaimed, to anyone in their family as well as themselves.

Pandemonium broke out as all the so called doubters charged to line up in front of my meager self. Remember that these souls averaged an age of 65 years and did posses many ailments.

Well after performing as I had promised, I humbly asked if they were now true believers in God and the Church He had established through His Son Jesus Christ? They all sounded like a cores of Angels with their heart felt, thankfulness.

After much consoling and cajoling I finally got them all to relax, and quieted down. I then began to explain to them that I would try to accomplish the theory that I had proclaimed to our Lord.

Concluding with a question, I asked, "Now that you all believe and understand my plight, I would definitely appreciate your feedback. What do you think would be the best way to convince the entire world of God's love for us and our best way to actually serve Him, here on earth?"

After numerous suggestions, some trivial, some outrageous and some just plain dumb, we came upon one that seemed to have potential. After discussing further, we came upon one. It was a compilation of various proposals and one that I personally had liked. This was our plan.

We would first designate 12 followers to accompany me on my travels, as Jesus Christ had done. We would travel all over the world using all of todays best technologies such as planes, boats etc. We would designate another three intellectual types who would prefer staying home, to be our secretaries, (with the help of their wives, hopefully), and maintain a constant record of our world wide experiences, via lap top computers, which all would possess.

The first order of business would be to have the monetary funds to accomplish this. Here I suggested would be the time for me to pick the 5 plus 1 in the N.Y. state mega million dollar game, which would take place tomorrow night. The current jackpot prize was listed as 90 Million.

And so I walked right out of the club and went across the street to the candy store. I took a Mega Million Play sheet and secretly listed the numbers on my play card. After the proprietor ran my play card through the machine, I took the ticket and hid it in my wallet. The play sheet which was returned to me I lit to flame as I also fired up a cigarette.

I returned to the club where I continued to plan our days ahead with my friends...............

Session Nineteen

Well here I finally am again. I really don't know how long it has been since my last encounter with the keys. I presume, about two years. I know my little, fictitious tale which precedes this writing may have caused some excitement in the reader and do fervently apologize for same. The reason being that I will not continue with it, but rather continue with my personal bio.

It is presently October of 2004, and I have attained, (with the grace of God), the ripe old age of 65. I am whole heatedly grateful to the Lord for this honor.

So many things have transpired since my last writing that I find it hard to list them. First and formats I must mention that about a year ago I did go through a horrible and disabling bout of depression gain, which lasted about 6 months. I'm sure the reader can understand me not mentioning it further.

Instead I'll just mention all the wonderful people I knew who died and are now hopefully with God. Most recent is Bo-Bo Forcerelli, Florinda Lentini, Sonny Mc Graw and my beloved Uncle Louie. Over these last few years since my last writing lots of things have changed. My wife and I did finally find a fine abode, after almost 2 years of living like vagabonds. This I must say was largely due to the efforts of my older son Joey. I can remember my old friend Father Bob Bannome exclaiming to me " you never know, God gave him to you for something great". Boy he certainly came through for my wife and I. We now live in a wonderful apartment in Yonkers. It's a ground level 2 bedroom place, with an out door patio, with umbrella table and chairs, Char cole grill and all the God given ambiance of beautiful foliage and trees, all maintained by the maintenance crews.

My friend Peter also went through some very hard times during this period as well. He under went two heart operations and lost his wife, Barbara during this ordeal. I prayed ardently for him and thank God for having spared one of my best friends.

Lets see, I think I should get off these depressing things and get back to myself, which is what this story is supposed to be about. Hopefully I don't sound too vain saying so.

Session twenty

I'd like to explain now about the times in my life when I was in the corps and my mean side did expose itself. For the sake of my Grand son and my other family members, let me state here that I was never the type who considered himself a wise or tough guy. But there are times in life when you have to stand up for weaker people, especially against bully's.

One night while at advanced infantry training in N.C. at Camp Lejune, my company was on night maneuvers in the boondocks. When we finished we marched back to the Quonset huts where we slept. Well it was about 12:30 am and we had to clean our weapons before we could go to sleep.

We did this as expeditiously as we could since 5am our wake up cal was not too far off. Well it was about 1am when we finally hit the rack. Just at this time the barracks bully decided to start a loud boisterous conversation with his flunkies on the other side of the barracks. No one uttered a word, until I got real discussed and called out, "hey pal, how about keeping it down, so we can get a few hours sleep." Well he answered me with real foul language and threats. After I answered and received the same type of verbal abuse, I slipped off my bunk clad only in my scivy shorts, and tip toed across the dark squadbays concrete floor. When I reached the bed of the bully, who was in the top bunk. I grabbed him around his neck with both hands and pulled him off the bed onto the floor and on his back. I then proceeded to pummel him with punches while he was down. This I did cause I feared he would get up and harm me. After all he was a large stocky guy. Well when someone turned on the lights I found my white scivvy shorts covered in red blood, as was all of the floor and the bully who was unconscious.

I slept good that night and when I got up and exited the squad bay, who do you think I encounted? Yes, the bully, who proclaimed to me. "Hi Ya!". End of that story. I'll continue with another at my next key board encounter, which I hope will be soon.

Session Twenty One

Well looka here it is, soon. Its now Sunday October 31St. 2004, Halloween. I've just completed reading another book. This one was very inspiration and made me feel happy with myself and in the mood to write. The book was called "Rise, Let Us Be On Our Way", by John Paul II. I do highly recommend it.

My next encounter with a big and I mean big, bully was one night when we were in a big squad bay in Okinawa. I was with the 9th Marines, then and when we weren't in the field, we were housed in these Army barracks. We were the only Marines who relished these fine barracks. All other Marine outfits on the Island were hosed in quwansit huts. I found out later that the reason for this was, that in the event of any hostilities in the far East, Our 9th. Marines would be the first ones in. Boy was I glad that I didn't listen to a buddy of mine who tried to persuade me to re up when my 3 year tour was up. Later When the Vietnam war was in full swing I happened to read a "Time" magazine. And low and behold who do you think I saw a picture of, prominently pictured with a bandoleer of ammo around his neck, holding an M60? It was my old pal, Robert E. Lee Cotton, the black guy who wanted me to ship over and be with him. We became very close because he was my tent mate when we were in the field. When we were in barracks and able to have Liberty call, he was always at a judo and karate class in town, which the Company would pay for. He became a black belt at it, and was real tough. Me I would always be in town for the females.

Getting back to the barracks. The lights were out and all in their racks were trying to call upon the sand man, when all of a sudden this big guy comes in drunk, and grabs this smaller guy out of his bunk and proceeds to pummel him with an excruciating beating. The beatee was screaming for his life with screeching wails. No one in the place seemed to say or do a thing. It was at this point I decided to try to break them up, before the big guy killed him. I proceeded to turn on the squad bay lights. I then pulled the big guy off the little. I then had my left hand affixed to his throat a while looking up at him I said "come on Rydell (or whatever his name was, I can't recall) your going to hurt this guy and get yourself in trouble." With this he grabbed my left arm with a free right hand and while exerting great pressure on my arm he growled at me, something to the effect that he would kill me. That's all I had to hear, my heart raced with fear and I instinctively brought my right fist back and then forward to his jaw with all my mite. I never realized how potent my right was until that night because the guy never woke up until the next day.

The next day, boy was that a day. We had mustered outside the barracks and were waiting for a sergeant to march us to chow. Well I was in the center of 3 files, the short guys in front, the mediums in center and the big guys in the 3rd and rear file. We were at ease and some guys were talking. As I just stood there I herd from right behind me, this guy saying, "man, somebody hit me last night and when I find him". Before he said another word I fearfully turn around, saw him rubbing his chin and said "It was me Rydell, you were looking to kill that kid, if you want to still fight me I will?", he mercifully said, "Oh!, Joe I didn't know it was you, thanks, I could've really gotten in trouble." Boy you know I said a prayer of thanks to the Lord after that reply.

I've had quite a few other scrapes in the service as well as in civilian life. I never got hurt but must admit I did get beat once. I would be a coward if I didn't mention it, if for nothing else but to prove humility is a condition of life.

I walked in the barracks one day and a few guys approached me saying that they knew who stole my spare boots, which were missing for a few days. They brought him in front of me and I looked down and there on his feet were my boots. The boots I loved which I had made a 150 mile, in 5 days hike. Well, I was mortified and proceeded to take off my shirt and proclaim to him, that I was going to break his ass. He kept saying he didn't want to fight and he was sorry. He made me sorry to have to act like this. I told him if he would have asked me I would have lent them to him. But as I was saying this, all the guys around were screaming for blood and cajoling me to hit him. This I finally did. I hit him with a short, quick, left and right to the face, which later produced a colored mouse on his eye. He then proceeded to charge me and wrapped his arms completely around me and threw me to the ground. He held me in that vise grip until I desperately tried to wiggle out of it, and couldn't. All the guys were screaming "come on Joe get him" And just the ordinary Joe that I was, I completely exhausted myself trying to get free. But to no Avail. Now that was a real humbling experience for me. Always remember that your not as, strong, tough, smart, rich, good-looking, etc. as you may think, only as good as God wishes you to be.

Session Twenty Two

Here I am again, only about a week since my last encounter at the keys. It's Sunday morning at 1:07 am, on Nov. 7th., 2004

After some deliberation, I've come to the conclusion that I will not go on any further with this my bio. I know I said originally that It would just go on until my death, and then be left as a legacy for my family, especially my grand children. But after speaking with my Aunt Jeanne, who read a part of it. I was convinced to try and have it published. Who knows we might make some money from it. I feel that God is also propelling me to do so.

Before I do anything else though, I will first have it proof read by my granddaughter Amanda, who's abilities I have complete faith in. Afterwards I'll see how many pages we can get out of it and then submit it to a publisher.

And so this will be my last night at the keys for my bio, which I've often said. It makes me feel almost sorry to part with it, but I truly feel God inspiring me to do so, and then I don't feel so bad.

I would like to end my piece with the following....

Since my wife and I moved to our new abode here in Yonkers,N.Y. we had the opportunity to change our parish of worship. We are now members of the Saint John's Church. At this church I usually frequent the 5P.M. mass on Saturday Evenings. At this mass the Pastor of the Church always says the mass. His name is Msgr. J. Christopher Maloney. To me he is the best preacher of the words of God, that I have ever heard. His explanation of all the Gospels are so clear, precise and understanding. In fact last Saturday I started bringing my mini tape recorder to tape his sermons. This was the second week I did so, and it was at Church while listening to his words that I definitely decided to end this my chatter. I have decided to end my bio with this his sermon I heard tonight. It was from a Gospel by Luke pertaining to death and resurrection. I wish the reader, could have herd it in his melodious voice, but here goes:-

Session Twenty Three

"My friends, the central theme of today's liturgy is clearly resurrection and life eternal. Belief in the resurrection of the body and life ever lasting is at the core of the Christian faith, and has been from the beginning. But we don't speak much about it, except at funerals, and we don't hear too many sermons about it either. Our religious life is often caught up in moral questions, ethical problems, social justice issues, matters of Liturgy, or Church practice. When religious conversation occurs among Catholics the subject are usually about the Churches position on the celibate clergy, or Capital punishment, abortion or gay marriage. One seldom hears a discussion about the resurrection of the body or eternal life in Heaven. However understandable that may be, it is also true that for any traveler, the most important question is WHERE ARE YOU GOING? So if our life on earth can be compared to a journey, then the way we make that journey, the things we value, the things we spend time and money and energy on, should reflect our answer to the basic question, does our life journey have a purpose, a direction? If so? What is it? Where are we going? When we're young and strong it can be easy to forget that life is a temporary thing. But, ever since Sept. 11th., all of us young or old, strong or weak, all of us have been given a powerful and unforgettable lesson as to how fragile and vulnerable we are. "Mamento Morea," the Ancients used to say. "Mamento Morea", Remember Death. Now there is some people that think that talking about death is depressing, but, Christians who are surrounded by images of the cross understand that it is just plain foolish to try to escape the inevitability of death. The Cross is central to Christian life and Christian thought, and the Cross teaches us that death does not have to be feared, once we realize that death is not an end. Its a transition. The last stage of a journey that takes us from this life, into the life to come. Perhaps that is why Christians can understand how St. Francis of Assi could welcome the arrival of the one that He called brother death. Yes death involves a separation from our body, from our friends and family, from this good earth. The uncertainty of death highlights the mystery of life itself, a mystery that is often covered up by the business, by the clutter of daily living that often prevents us from looking at or spending time with the mystery of our inner selves, the place where we can really be alone with God. But in spite of all of life's precious distraction, we can still experience a kind of restlessness. A sense that there is more to human experience, than even the greatest human joys can provide. A restlessness that Saint Agustine acknowledged, when he wrote. The heart is restless, until it rests, in God. There are two fundamental texts in the new testament, that discuss the life of the world to come. The first is in St. Paul's 1st. letter to the Corinthians. Chapter II, tells us, "I have not seen, nor ear herd, nor has it entered into the human heart, what God has prepared for those who love Him." The second text is in the 3rd chapter of the 1st. letter of St. John, where we read, "Beloved, we are Gods children now, what we shall be has not yet been revealed, when it comes to light we shall be like Him, who we shall see Him as He Is." Theologians call the happiness in Heaven, the Beatific Vision. What that means, I think, is simply this. Somehow when we enter Heaven, the presents of Gods glory and Gods goodness envelopes us, it floods our minds and our hearts with so much joy that it radiates through our entire being. And we experience perfect joy. All our desires, will be fulfilled, all our questions answered, all our dreams realized. We can't be precisely sure what Heaven will be like, but, this much we know. It will be better and it will be more than we can imagine. How we believe in the life of the world to come reinforces our commitment to value life here on earth, because we see this life as having ultimate meaning and purpose. Our belief in the life to come, reinforces our efforts to do battle against the powers of evil, described by St. Paul in today's second reading. To do battle against whatever would diminish life, or deform the body or demean the soul. Our belief in the future helps us to value the present. Because it is in the present that we prepare for the future, which is another way of saying, that the life of the world to come begins here and now. In this life, in this world. Our life in Christ, has begun here, it will reach its fulfillment in the next world, but that fulfillment will simply extend and complete what we already experience here on earth. In prayer, in the sacraments and most especially in the sacrament of the Ehucarist. Because it is there in the Ehucarist that Jesus tells us, if you eat My flesh and drink My blood, you shall have my life within you. At every Ehucarist we renew that life within us. As we listen to the Gospel of the Lord and renew our commitment to living that Gospel. If we live the life of Jesus Christ, if we make our journey with Him, than when it comes to the end and we stand before God in judgment, we won't come to a place where we feel strange or akward or afraid or out of place. Heaven see, is the answer to the question we started out with. Where are you going? Heaven is the place God designed us for, we won't be surprised when we feel comfortable there, we should feel comfortable there, cause its our HOME.

The End

About the Author

Reading the book would provide a full canvas of the author's life.

His trials and tribulations, his loves and disappointments, and finally his future hopes, are all there for the reader to savor.

Listing some here would be redundant.